THE SIN EATER

DEBORAH RANDALL

The Sin Eater

BLOODAXE BOOKS

ISBN: 1 85224 041 5

First published 1989 by
Bloodaxe Books Ltd,
P.O. Box 1SN,
Newcastle upon Tyne NE99 1SN.

Bloodaxe Books Ltd acknowledges
the financial assistance of Northern Arts.

Typesetting by Bryan Williamson, Manchester.

Printed in Great Britain by
Bell & Bain Limited, Glasgow, Scotland.

With love do I seek
my children, born strangers.

Acknowledgements

Acknowledgements are due to the editors of the following publications in which some of these poems first appeared: *Aireings, The Gregory Poems 1985-1986* (Penguin Books/Society of Authors, 1987), *Iron, Poetry Book Society Anthology 1988/89* (Hutchinson/ PBS, 1988), *Poetry with an Edge* (Bloodaxe Books, 1988), *Sheaf,* and *The Wide Skirt.*

The Sin Eater was the winning collection in the Bloodaxe national poetry competition in 1987. 'Danda with a Dead Fish' won first prize in the 1987 Bridport poetry competition.

Contents

The Sin Eater

It might be missed,
lovesick and bovine

above the here-to-nowhere grin,
and there, another.

It might be a baby
in a pickling jar,

far cry
from a cuddle.

Christ stood on Her when he walked on water.

Blood is what blood is,
even peculiar to flies and fishes.

Christ's blood is drunk in holy ritual,
and thus the ocean toasts her too.

He made Them in his image,

to receive the wound
and wonder at it.

And thus the world was saved by victims.

He made her soft-contoured,
womanly.

She gives milk.

He made her a measly eye in a mountain,
fashioned for compassion,

and a massive cheek to turn.

An eye to trap His image
unforgiven.

Danda with a Dead Fish

Here is Danda with a dead fish,
this boy has too many limbs it seems,
more spindles than his running stitch can handle,
in from the green-flax sea-line with bare legs
and his knees clacking, chattering Danda
with a dead fish, what it is and whether fresh
or not they'll pass it over, won't know,
won't eat it she says, though you my dearie
Danda can have it for your supper, how
she teases, his big mother, navvie-built
to be a father; where do all the men go
when they have begot.

Don't look so starving Danda you
little darling, who packs his food away
like a navvie and is growing all slick
and silvery and smells kippery, he's been
hull-picking with fishermen, his father was
one of them, nets going mouldy, Danda
gets moods of the sea, and goose-bumps
can't be scraped off, he'll get them again
on the shore, he lives there looking for
the man in him, they give
tea and talk, slap him on the shoulder,
call him fishy.

Danda's jumper unravelling, coming out
in sympathy, his nose is never cleanly,
dripping brine all the time, scales under
his nails, always flexing, finding, bringing
in, a wind slaps hard on him singing up and
down his ribs, Danda has no colour
except of grey, the colour of
the day he lost his fiery ginger dadda
to the sea, except, his dadda really went away
with a woman not his mother;
never mind our Danda, pass it over
have your supper.

The Impossible Death Scream of the Unpalatable Pike

A thing caught under
impossible to reel in
or bring up
out of the mouth
out of the shining shattered face.

Spatter the glassy smile to spray
which may be tears
except tears don't cut any ice underwater.

Fly-fishing
running with my line
except this time
he erupted a pike
an explosion in our marriage
a mine.

My tongue on a hook
the impossible death scream of the unpalatable pike.

Nightwatchman

Brother nightwatchman I have shared your way,
black upon black footfall upon the crazily paved street
and eyes and hands full of each other so drunk
the wine to vinegar as we walk without talk on my tongue
and hands feeling for ourselves as only strangers can,

the lock and the alien roof and the fumble for them
unseemly unhomely things that we build about ourselves
after marriages have broken I still dream of eggs bitter
and raw such as my father slid down his throat at dawn,
falling from my fingers so much rage still to come,

I don't remember a time in two years when alcohol
wasn't wailing in my veins, a substitute for tears
like the grab and grind with a new nightwatchman,
the surprising angle of the apple in your throat
the lotion in your skin, you don't smell like him,

stairs are unholy alliances, every one and many
sneaking under the soles of our feet the squeak
of female philandering as I size the nightwatchman's shoulders
estimate the blades in there and how they shall
rub for pleasure under my hands two wishbones wondering,

the door is the single hymen I have to admit you
and you ahead owning me and my womb without name
flicking your beautiful hair gold and white and shampoo
and I live alone, lone as the furthest star that cannot
be seen, little girl frantically signalling,

nightwatchman on my carpet you are so naked, and proud
as a pose, I have watched this maleness, I see in the dark
and I know, and I'm tired, tired of the drumskin belly
the random muscle below, a perilous house of cards
is building in me, my history frail and impersonal,

the neon snakes of your arms nightwatchman
wind and wind about me and the carpet rolls us up
and the solitary bed is empty our flesh on the floor
in choreography, and a neighbour rapping his fifty year old
indignation, an accompaniment to my game,

I open my four lips for your fingertips and my cunt weeps
as my face won't, and like an angry sponge absorbs you,
all, and when you are sleeping I watch the night,
small boys sleep off their pleasure, I watch
the night, and wonder at such perfect death.

An Amsterdam Garden

When I was young I was a Merchant Seaman,
that's how I came to be sleeping with a very disturbed
Dutch woman who'd been left by her husband in the marital home.

I stood at her picture window admiring her garden,
she was using sex at that time as a metaphor.
Get back to bed, she said. She spoke perfect English.

Her cheese-coloured hair ran over the pillow.
Strange thoughts entered my mind just then
of the home and people I'd left behind, the nice girl
who didn't know I was cheating (they dish out antibiotics
like sweeties in the Merchant Navy).

My dad forever reading a paper, black-and-white life
coming off in his fingers, my mum I'd never known
as a person, a younger brother and sister
to whom I was a nonentity.
Even a pet mongrel dog growing rickety.
Death seemed imminent at home.

The depressing nature of our coupling got to me,
her flawless skin like the sheets had made so many sailors.
She had a fun fur on the floor, a tiger skin,
and her pubic hair was manicured to a perfect heart,
tired old fur I thought.

There is a sickness comes on the mariner.
Going round the world a few times makes him dizzy
and so dislocated he'd mistake a whore for a mother,
maybe we only think two ways about women
but something was cracking in me, I wanted reality,
not to be another punter in another seaport city.

Hand me a cigarette, sailor. My beard has been growing
twelve hours or more. I'm staying the weekend, we're instant,
junk food intimates, she strikes my chin for a light,
I hate women who smoke. I smile and kiss her.

14

Her lips are clutching, even barnacles look for something
and cling, I understand, I want to go home, just as
she wants him, her husband again. I float
on my back in their wide blue marital bed
that lets the ocean in.

Something is cracking.

Gulls in their thousands are screaming for scraps
all over the world, following the fool and his money.
I am just another stranger who enters her body,
entertains for a while and is gone. She must believe
I am special, I am the one, she is lonely.
And after we're over horizons, she's empty.

She's someone's daughter, someone's wife, who knows,
someone's mother, these are the structures that lend support
and mean the most, someone to love and forgive.
We haven't given, only flesh in collision,
an imitation of the real thing, we haven't really
cared for ourselves. She showed me how to go home.

I want to belong.

The tulips I got her from the garden and gave her
have a centre, which is the fibrillator of the heart,
and now they drop their dust, the old sea-rust
of goodbyes in their thousands.

Maelstrom

Seaweed jumble stacked along the shore after a swell,
the tide is almost out of sight and hence the sickening smell
of seabirds rotting, the ones caught by storm.
Remember we'd mixed together under an eiderdown
and heard nothing, except our mouths working.

A baby porpoise beached forever, shiny still
in his best bib and tucker, so utterly without defence.
And seemingly I shouldn't care you left me so soon after,
he was fighting for his life, I can't imagine
what forces sent him to this wreck and ruin
while we were sleeping.

There are hurts by degree and these creatures
are most hurt, my heart survives, it is beating, not beaten,
the cause of my animation, anemones like hearts
have been thrown up, and small jellyfish that had no bones
to be broken, but they do not live.

Your child rides inside me against the world,
and you are careless of that fact, cool as Nature,
or a patriarchal God, imitating partiality
in the act of creation, I know your sperm were random.
I know life must cherish life through woman.

Sea Cow

I put my baby to your chest,
pulsing pink anemone mouth
kneading for your nipple,
you shrank from the unexpected
sting, a mere stipple, scarcely
grasped, amongst your male
fronds and your flat male treasury
that could not be breached
for milk or martyrdom.
Lady Macbeth in the underworld,
I'd bash the brains from my baby,
that squib, as if the glutty
mouth and hermit-crab head could
be cracked for tender meat, a treat.
My baby is beached on your chest,
all jelly and cuttle,
a damp squid, and if I could
I would have your nipple jet
milk and my baby suckered
there while I grew careless
mermaid's hair and a mermaid's
happy tail, no more to be
eroded or exploded, a silver
whiplash muscle to drive,
where I have been driven
by your muscle, which is coral
and irresistible to this.

Schoolboys in the Sea

'He went into the sea with a swimming party and was never seen again.'

Imagine not growing to manhood Alisdair
and something in the City.

How deeply you have delved
and we know nothing.

Your mother came with a funeral face
she wore weeds and forget-me-knots
in her stockings.
She turns a lovely leg Alisdair
your mother, her beauty unleashed
our lust where have you been keeping her?
She wore heather
a long way from Galloway
to cast after you on the water.

The grass air-brushed that day
blade by blade smouldering in the heat,
we found a ploughman's old lump of cheese
many weathers hard in a pleat.

Last down the cliff path
we two nattering as usual,
the sea crooned lazily
only a shushing to sleep on the shelves
only a smattering of sun on the water.

Then we swam naked
white schools of boys
tossing and teasing like fishes.
The heat fizzed out of our skin
as we went under, born again
through cool green conception.

Imagine crabs mustering on their claws
scrimshawing bones
crimped hair colours
lazily out let
mermaids blew kisses
filled our mouths with bubbles.

Alisdair I held you down
your face became the waning moon
dissolving like a Sunday wafer.

Imagine you knowing
how it feels to drown
as if a tear had overcome you.

Your cap clung to its peg a whole year after Alisdair
and when no one missed you I wore it to remember.

Gavin

I suppose you don't tire ever of looking over to Skye,
a mean man, and mean mountains, but they imply
the spirit stripped to necessity.

Whisky thick as morning pee,
and a tang on your tongue when you let me kiss.

Man and boy, and animal, and vegetable, and mineral,
they spin to joy, how you felt
when you made the world this.

Quirky little spirit, in reversed aspic,
a burn like mercury,
mercurial the smile, unbestowed but lurking.

I saw you go with the first fag of the day,
basted by the juices of first light,
unhuman things at your feet.

The beach is love, is virgin skin, stretched out
for a hammering.

Behind shades in the Hebrides,
to keep your eyes in.

I shook hands the first time,
a hand that was sleeping seagull,
the sea came off on me, the saturation,
the power and the passion.

Close, you smelled of ashes.

The light gets through the sky somehow,
I remember you in all shades of grey.

Your private eyes, when you stripped for me.

So suddenly there, so suddenly not.

My ear pressed to your chest, I heard the sea,
what words can't be
and animals are.

The creature comfort we take in one another,
I couple but you were rutting.

Pick a shell, any shell,
feel it tremble,
sound as a bell, it has been to sea
an empty vessel.

That is my blood dripping from your rowan tree
on your head, making rust.

Put up the big rock now.
I sent curses when I meant love.

Even your handful of dust you have sealed from me
lest you run through my fingers
when I embrace you, unspeakably.

Longships and Lovers

Lift the lovely truth and let it have a breath.
Thori spins words and they stick in my craw like sheep floss,
he's bloody and predictable.
What is between us but blackness,
look into my eyes at war for this truth
to which I attach most meaning.

So we shared a sword and a high friendship
and latterly, unwillingly, a woman.
You know I'd have put my back against you
and given as many lives as one had I possessed them
to your honour and preservation.
You are a fine Earl, men speak of you across oceans
and I'm going to kill you.

With love I will kill you
softly as the speaking bird insinuating a talon
into the breast of a rival.
I don't want to hurt you, I have seen you naked and young
in a river, I know what you built your manhood on,
snowy flesh that kept a purity.

Your worst mistake was misjudgement.
They grow careless in high places,
envy might be a gnat-bite not worth consideration.
You were so sure of her you weren't often there,
so secure in me you left us together.
Shall I tell you what I have tasted?

I am preparing for war, it is in my blood
singing and there's nothing I can do,
we were made for this above beauty and truth
to kill. I am lascivious
with war, shoulder to shoulder we have despatched.
I want her less, I will have you,
I must have your head and look into your eyes
after death.

Thori maddens me, he sees the hag on my shoulder.
It ends badly

but so this world we know shall end
muffled into sanctity. I have sniffed the new climate,
the sops that gladly put their hearts on our swords,
the stones they raise up in some remote place to His glory.

When you look at me after death
hanging from my hand I think you ended well,
you bind me up with crimson cords down my arm.
I live by vengeance.
The lovely truth is not pretty
I have become the sea-wolf that turns on his own
I don't even trust myself
my right hand might do the deed while I sleep.

Your brothers come for me,
it will not be a healthy end, Thori was right
but I sought it, I wanted it for us both
this world is not a fit place for a warrior.
I didn't tell you in time about the sickness
on me after we had returned from our last raid.
Killing had lost its savour.

A strange fear gripped
in the region of the heart,
I shook and could not sleep it away.
You thought I had caught swamp-fever remember.
What can I say without shame.
I saw through our prescribed way
there was a gentleness in me, a desire to spare life.
I even wanted to give,
I feared I was becoming a woman or worse a Christian.
Killing had never brought any of this into question.

I took your life to know the truth.
The truth is it was a sin.
I challenged myself to do it
to exorcise a dream of peace. I believed in killing,
it was action, it was good clean fun.
It made me more than a man, I could overcome death.
At your last breath I knew what I had done
and I fear now that if your brothers find me
they will send me to heaven. Only
Thori says that we shall never meet again.

Culloden
Donuil na Braiteach

They threw stones.
His body bound by colours he ran
hither and thither he knew not where.
A retreat galls hot blood
so friend and kinsman stood
fifteen paces from the line
scorning the sword for the stone
until death dismissed them...

Carry the colours home
in time he came home
his sons Charles and Angus
daubed after the deed,
fame carries on their shoulders
squarer than the next man
lest the next man should question
the begetting of them,
how their father turned fear to account...

They fell in droves
the good wild drovers
who lived under sky more often than wood
who grew thick skin
to keep at bay the early winters
explain the clan to Cumberland
brother with brother they stood
inbred to the last
they have pulled eagles out of the sky
seen eye to eye with the heather...

The Beast and Fiona

Fiona is cruel no doubt about it,
she affords her callousness and pays with youth and beauty,
we love best those careless creatures who torment us,
at least when they look as she does.

Fresh from an exchange visit to France's southern regions,
she has gorged on fat vines and erotic sun
and shall return just as soon as she's delivered
the kiss of dispatch to her aged lover.

And here he is on the heathery hill, their trysting place,
an hour he's waited in cold and driving rain
for late Fiona, who picks her way, fine as a hart,
an arrogant twitch to her nose when she gets wind of him.

He's already miserable, she intended he should be,
water has got in and run him through to the heather,
he raises an arm to her like a drowning sailor,
but she's thinking of Pierre.

Fiona has a ticklish way of touch, a tease put in,
she can't resist hot meanings for they enhance
her reputation though she's against gentle dealing
and reclaims her perfect chin from his kiss where he missed.

She plants a last perfunctory one on him
then walks away, she doesn't linger but does display
her pretty haunches, she can't resist it,
to leave him in a lather, old enough to be her father.

Each fingerprint she left on his hide is washed away,
only a whiff of his carnal self clings under his Barbour.
Indelible as ever, he sets his deerstalker at a less jaunty angle,
the decrepit stag so nearly gave himself to the gun.

Reasons for Falling

Murdo the mad sheep-minder went toward heaven
his notched machete carved a niche in Cairngorm winter
and his human flesh took hiding under fleece and leather
to fool his maker.

He's already lived forever
is yet to be found set hard in mid-breath
asking only a boulder for his head.
Murdo spurns every man's bed
lest comfort take hold,
at least he could walk the red peculiar grit
picked up in a lifetime
up a mountain.

Murdo and an eagle enjoyed brotherhood,
sentiment was spit to them
and Murdo admired the cheek of the devil
as he watched his lambs go flying.
This eagle defies the order of things
to raise the humble creature.

Murdo the mad sheep-minder went toward heaven
his notched rifle cut a swath in Cairngorm winter
and he nods to his maker
conscious of a job well done.

The Hare

The hare might almost be a concept
but is beyond thought,
quick as a cream-tailed comet,
mute as the colour brown.

The hare strips lychetts,
is blunt and gangling in play
but with a flick and a twist
leads the hounds of hell astray
over cliffs.

Pendulum-bellied cows munch ear-of-hare,
they tread hare in but hare is spring
and surfaces again further up the field.
The hare paddles the field, against
the grain of the grass.

The hare's ears swivel in weather-vanes,
register thunder, echo-sound shoals of wind,
an armada gathering in the channel.
The hare's nose tastes the many strains of air.

The hare's fur is hyperactive
and untouched in a lifetime,
soft and mysterious as moleskin,
fast as fluid.

The hare's eyes are subterranean,
earth made them,
the grass laps their glassy balls
and drowns them.

The hare is a blood-song,
a song in the blood, a shivering
up and down the spine, from a time before
words outsped their meaning.

Chasing a Lark on Warbarrow Down

I have let my dog loose for a lark,
and he goes over the rim of the world,
in flight from the world.

Everything depends on an axis,
think beyond this atmsophere,
behind that star.

Wall of death in my blood today,
I am candy floss, dervish,
sustaining and defying gravity.

Life emanates from me,
how lonely the godhead,
how in need of worship.

My dog and I have unbecome,
lost to each other,
lost to the world.

Never again shall I wear my flesh mutely
or mortally sleep.

Horse

My old horse mumbles with his mouth.
He is a structure with rawhide pulled over.
Life has used him to death.

He is up to his frayed fetlocks
in a sinking field.
His lips are kind and skim an apple
from my hand.
His belly has slipped low to the ground.

His lips are a soft toy in my hand.
I hear the apple grinding
and his soft soft heart in servitude
beating to death.

We are both caught in the rain.

His tail slops.
It is a mop unravelling.
I close my hand on his breath.
A held field.

He is an old horse.
He was the apple tree I climbed
as a child.
He carried me.

We are both caught in the rain.

The Swans at Abbotsbury

A hurricane of wings in darkness unrelieved,
swans are leaving, the ship of fools pitches
and our hammocks collide.

To be a protected species, migrate at will
out of one life, or listen for everyday slops
under the rib of our ship. I have
a how-to-problem, how to be angry.

How come the night plugs my husband's
consciousness, his eyes, ears, tongue;
stowaway, he swings with my life
to tidal rhythms, a cabin boy again.

Don't, lovely swans, leave me, the most free thing
I lifted my eyes to. I could have learned from you,
from your wings' delicacy, said to be capable
of breaking a man's embrace.

Horizons become obscured at night
after the most pure sun has suffused the sea.
I feel it, the sickness on the weary mariner
who sails as a passenger, rocks passively.

Unright, unwrong, and that is why I long
for the storm, for lust to revisit me
or babies to be born, bursting bloody
for song or silence, it's all the same.

Argosy, a ship like a filled womb, sitting
deep in the water, wallowing home, port to port.
We call them our own, I swab and swab
my babies' bottoms, my husband's collars, my eyes.

Phosphorescence is beguiling. I shook it
from my hair, learnt to play a comb, to lullaby,
to live by choreography. Swans are deserting
the swannery at Abbotsbury, monk-made by men
jealous for consummation, a wing's whim,
and they cover oceans, avoiding a consuming death.

Wood Nymph

And this, he said, is the natterjack toad,
an obscene living fungus or a pregnant wart,
the sort of tongue you could pull and pull,
like the insides of a golf ball.

She took it in her hand, it lumbered off,
he scratched at the mosquito bites
under his shirt, the sort of shirt
lumberjacks wear, with the sleeves rolled manfully.

My favourite tree is the copper beech,
what's yours? he said, but she'd moved on
looking for something ugly,
and he watched the drift of her hair.

A white white blonde in the heart of the wood,
her hair took his breath away.
A spider swung over her path on silk,
she caught and crushed it casually,

and turned to him with an open hand
to show him what she had found.

'M'

Victim, victim, the plot screams.
Peroxide Pauline plays up,
it takes a regular guy
like Norman Mailer
to put her in her place,
that is, back to bed.
A shot in the fanny should cure her.

What does it take for Chrissake
to prove intelligence,
to do the same thing
ten times better?
Looker and hooker.
She married a playwright in glasses.
Her arse is still a blancmange.

Stick to the baseball players
who always stick up for a girl,
keep a straight seam
on a stocking,
and smile, smile,
resolutely wearing
no knickers.

The telephone is no cure
for feminine wiles,
neuter to her simper.
It isn't male.
Testosterone by trade
will let you down one day
just like old age.
Ring your momma,
if you're lucky enough to have one,
if she's still alive.
She loves you more than God or man.

Dolls come in many guises,
articulated,
rarely articulate,
the ideal pretty companion,
they give you kisses,
you can move their legs
and arms.
They even come flat
and inflatable.

This doll hangs on the telephone,
her plastic is showing.
Most guys don't mind that
but her plastic is showing,
her eyes have spilled.
Operator
the train is coming.
She's tied to the line,
it's Norma Jean,
acting again
Momma.

Claudia

Claudia, there are endless night-trains and tracks smacking
over the beat of your heart and stations
slamming in the dark
and I know you're not sleeping, your freckled back
is as clear as that endless fact.
Across Europe there are endless night-trains
and corridors shaking and I imagine myself in sleepwalk
trying to leave you and I imagine your back.
I want to touch your back
I thought I owned it and you slept
without clothes for me.
What must the look of your heart be like
behind breasts that are small fruits and tart nipples
a discontented organ indeed.
I am hugged in this sway of carriage and convey
caught in a drama and a dream of a European crossing.
Claudia I'll tell you something,
I'll speak in the language we keep for each other
or maybe hold my tongue.
I never left my coat tonight
still buckled tight and cold.
You wore black for passion and white
with your Hamburg husband and you return to him tonight
giving up flirtation and locomotion.
The endless shunt of your heart, playing with blood
I imagine, as you taught my blood to perform
with a passion.
Can I communicate my need to you the perfect bilingual
to make love to me for one last time to the tune of a train.
Claudia sleeping.
Understand this, I'm an Englishman, and all my life
I carry a dull sense of my own destination.

Catriona

So, baby, without the big buck deer that started up
you'd never have clung, the conifers closed, O,
they gave off a thicket smell, we might have rolled
on a bed of needle. It isn't easy to see the deer
disappear and to feel your startled clinging
come apart to curiosity.

You are frail-faced and wrapped in red polythene
like a plush tomato in its skin, and the big rain
spits derision and you zip up. You zip up.
The rain in the pines, only a stray smattering
of your darling hair left behind, as you pull on the drawstring.

Emma Answers Back

Guess how much I hated my husband,
the rat.

Seasons amend our lives girls.
Be warned.

Charm failed me.

His sweet eye was hooded,
I did not see how it roved.

There is lust in old leather.

He committed me to paper,
made an effigy.

He assuaged his guilt and fantasy,
his infidelities between the pages.

I slept alone though I was lusty.
I lived still as a stone.

He lived dry as a feather.

My wedding linen lies jaundiced
in some sick drawer.

He scratches over our life together,
leaves for the high cliff top to recover me.

But I am walled up alive in our rose-coloured bricks.
A true matron, I waited for death.

Truly what he made me.

He was an owl once but he's all right now

FRANCIS KILVERT:
*'One day Perch skinned an owl in London
and from midnight to one o'clock
he roamed about the streets seeking
where he might bestow the body of the owl
fearing that the carcase of the owl
might be found and described in the papers
as the body of a fine full-grown male child.'*

*

From midnight to one o'clock
an owl in London
roamed about the streets
seeking Perch.

From midnight to one o'clock
Perch skinned a fine full-grown male child
in London.

From one o'clock on
an owl with a talon for skinning
found Perch.

The papers described the carcase
as the body of a fine full-grown male child.

Or an owl.

It was obviously
a revenge tragedy
but as to identity
there was some confusion.

Holding

I need this, I am gourmand and you on a spike
returning the pain from day one when you struck deep
and drew raw, emotion runs red, loud.

O, the shout also spills, obscene from gut loin
and pure heart, must I present this organ pulsing,
saying 'love gorge' when lust for love trammels the tongue.

Spit out of these arms holding, I can match you child
blow by blow for asking, for fear to incubate a kiss,
for hunger, and only an eye to roll around the mouth.

Where were you anger? I wanted to lock this
receding lover, accuse this child, find in human history
a common cry for a creator.

Child give me mercy as you become mirage then
simmer into tears, the hours I have known tears boil and beg
and after, the empty room of you and I.

Lead me not to the tempest, with my two hands I usurp
your head, tousle my revenge down about your ears,
savage your dew cheeks for manna, look.

I am the orb of the world, hear me out,
the vanity that dreamed you into being, that can
release us, that destroys me for you.

Take me back to your embryo, curl placid in my belly,
give me peace and time to recreate you,
tell the sea to hold safe to the spinning orb.

Child you may have unmanned your mother, tame enough
under my wild hands, we matter both, symbiosis for another
life I promised you, for hope, look here.

You tore at my bread, you shed my wine,
the day of deliverance my life was laid down at your head,
dear head that I force up from my breasts to here.

Here we must part from one creature consuming itself.
If I open my hands and expect a butterfly, will you
impoverish my womb and make me fat.

This mother greed exudes her spring to wash you
as you explore her meaning, touching skull and lip
and sin, and hungering at last, hungering.

*Holding Therapy was developed in America and is a controversial
self-help method for the autistic child and his family.*

Don't Smack Me Again

Tomato hurt.
Tomato tight in hurt skin.
Hurt tomato red with held breath.
Red hurt tomato held tight in skin.
Hurt breath red with tomato.
Tight hurt tomato red.
Red skin in hurt tomato.
Held red tight with hurt breath.
Skin tomato tight with hurt held.
Hurt skin tight with tomato.
Hurt tomato.

Just the Girls to Cope

I wish I had been taught happiness
when I was much younger.
It came to me as a great surprise.

There were girls, my erroneous impression
that running a mental institution
they were just the girls to cope.
Impossible to say what was going on in their minds.

I couldn't foresee how brief the spell.
The blackhouse of sin came at midnight
and shocked me into returning to you
just as I had gone.

My visit to hotels as a stewardess
seems sick in retrospect.
I should have got some health in the Swiss Alps.
Troubles not over, I collected a pair of gloves.

And so it came to pass
I had to be taken out to pee
sweetly squatting in the grass
you pull my knickers up and down
just like a mummy.

41

The Strangeness of Silence

By the time this astonishing news broke
I had information that could lead us both to madness,

a Russian winter like a Bolshevik,
and Lewis of course is a bare island.

We ran out of toilet paper on the ninth day.
This frightened me out of my skin,

I would never have dreamed of speaking but
he unstopped my mouth, refused kisses.

The gulls came in battalions of hardened soldiers
making whoopee, whole reasons to listen above the din.

Watching a man and a woman cutting peats
they strain and grunt as if engaged in intimacy,

but this is better, it lies between respect
and distance, it's functional and free.

The cost is a photograph of me
looking like a dog's dinner.

I saw my first heron, a bird of breeding,
a good mechanic when it comes to fishing.

How perfect to support a desire, huffed out on husky winter air,
to unpick Russian dolls by the fire,

I was in tune with everything
except anger, anger is back home.

Art is the thing, I hate to live hatefully,
I could spit hot coals and hole the snow.

Aesthetic sin is, I hope, excusable
committed against a backdrop of buckets and harsh living.

Nothing is like an absence, absences give rise to talk.
I became attracted to the strangeness of silence.

Grandfather

I wonder why old age put a nappy on you,
why your eyes didn't age in their lunar landscape,
why your sense of humour came to fruition
on a felled tree. I wonder
about your hand, so inanimate a subject,
whether it held me or not at your last bed,
and whether your fingers heard what my mouth didn't say.

I remember how you couldn't cross a road straight,
how cars brought out the bullfighter in you.
I wish my dog had liked you better,
and my mother hadn't mothered you, because the boy
scuffled beside the soldier and your colours
weren't mixed right, so she dressed you
with her tongue, water on a duck's back.

I know you would have played truant
had you been at school.
You invented Canada in your seventieth year,
you took your stroke up the road to buy baccy.
You hid two wars where we couldn't find them,
you gave us humour in uniform,
you nicked your flagpole from the army.

I see you in a baby lately born.
She laughs like you and wears your ears for a joke,
she practises her parachute jumps too.
And I suppose when parachutes and loving hands can't
return you then the puff
of a few words like your interminable cloud
of pipesmoke must do.

Winter Kills
(for Mike Tomkies)

What manner of man lives out all year
besting the beasts who seek cover
or swim for it and flounder.

Images of a naked monk in winter,
his robe left like a hide
by the cracking water.

He'd rather turn blue than speak out
against the injustice of the red deer
so few this year.

See him passing prayers to the sky for exercise.
He knows every nuance of his feet stalking
until the snows came.

His thin yearning smoke sneaks out of the conifers,
brittle little lives collect about him
as if he imagined himself to be St Francis.

He'd rather not be seen alive with them
than dead with us.
We wait to trap him

but we didn't wait ten years in a wilderness
holding our breath,
the downwind of our breath.

He has brown inevitable eyes,
a knife to slip the joints,
the talent to turn to ice for enjoyment.

Suffer the red deer to come unto him
holy hunter,
their big eyes return him his due.

Leaving

We latched arms and went,
up, down, along the lane in rut,
antlers strutted in the hedgerows,
shed velvet.
I peeled velvet from a beechnut
and gave it to you.
Hardly touchable.
The year turned,
I vow it turned then.
The dark was coming in
and our breath went out, cold.

The lane without departure,
or destination, strung us along.
We walked on well-latched shoes.
Our talk became distant,
it fell like first snow
on closed ears.
Our eyes were dark,
they looked apart, blind words
began their migration.

I latched my coat against the cold
but it came through the earth through soles.
The crook of our two arms froze.
In the beechwood, silence,
savage with clattering leaves.
Hedgehogs soon must hibernate,
reel silence on their spines, turn in
and hoard themselves in a hug under trees.
The skin of the self is always best, will always be
an embraceable thing.

My Roaring Boy

My roaring boy comes home,
I hear him lungful across
the shifting corn, he scatters
the stooks and all before him, he is
bright as a cob's flank in June,
true as the ploughshare's chop
through the dark dark earth,
larger than the harvest moon
which is an owl's eye and cannot
lie and cannot deny his undoing
as the years fold and fold upon
themselves and his seed grows
to his overthrow and I do love him,
and he is, forever bright, forever
true, forever larger than the moon.
My boy comes roaring home.

A Presentation Clock

Rain again, nattering on the convoluted shed
where forced rhubarb under shards
grows blindly ahead of its time

and a presentation clock rocks on
the mantelpiece where china-eyed cats
squint through glaze cracked

in a map and colours of endurance
slide down panes and grandmother
with her pains grows old in the chair

and wallpaper shows its roses all year
and grandfather peels his paper
onto another page and dilates

his cataracts to see what's on
the box and his slippers in
their winter coat sleep on sleep on

and the coals in the grate
pep and glow and redden as
they soothe and die and somewhere

cabbage is boiling dry and crocuses
come in the garden and an ice cream van
on the horizon chuckles children away.

My Favourite Sunday

Old ladies in church hats remind me of giraffes,
something about gravity slipping chins down necks
always straining for the pulpit
in wet-look straw and raw crimplene,
a squabble in their throats
and bosoms with the massive swank of rhinoceros.

Old ladies in church hats remind me of lions,
a suggestion of puffy blue heads on the prowl,
or hyenas daubed round the mouth
an expression of just having eaten a carcass.

White old ladies and that great white hunter
the vicar, on safari together,
it was invariably the young and the weak
he sniped for over the sepulchre
as we lay between the pews and played dead.

My favourite Sunday was the Sunday I chose
never to go to church again
until I was old and wanted to be
eighty per cent of the church congregation
and my own salvation then I suppose
would seem more imperative,
could no longer be said to be more
synonymous with survival.

Other People Also Burn Wood

He slides an eye brimful
with the best about lovers,
somewhere over my shoulder.

I want to recall my hands
getting toasted on his sensed
flame which is so far real

not gas with mock fall-out.
I smell incendiary wood on him
which gives me a crackle

in unmentionable memorable places.
Strangers only, meet in my eye
as if it were a market-place

where they auction the business
of the day, or a pub yawning
on New Year's morning.

He's in my eye
talking in an office sort of way
not really

really looking here
but somewhere over my shoulder
where a chosen lover

tends the fire.

Going into the Sea

Why don't you make something easy, dear God?
For instance make fish speak

lashed on the slab,
make them ask for water.

Make colours of fish more than a handful of silver
and fast in the sea.

Undo my death before it happens
I am greedy.

Fisher hands of my fisher friends
reach me.

I've found out who your Jonah was
dear God.

Only by acts of uneasiness and imperfection
do we live

like Judas
slinging belief after treachery.

Questo

(or Never Take Sweets from a Stranger)

An Palfrey pottered outen on the playne,
Burdened all down under the buttum
Of hys Lady-large who seeken for her Knight,
(Ger'ain't a Knight in fayre England
But hym afright frum her.) Right? Questo!

Her cummen atten trot unto
An greeny wood, de Lady she espy
An drageroony casten all in ey
And cloven feeted, sleepering.
Thaughten she to pass, ah fol
De rol, ol' drageroony waks.

Nun yet dismayed this lang-synce mayde
Withdrawen discreetish to an dystant
Glayde, tho drageroony heem pursue
To sayen all halloo, but much ado
When her, hym she got wynd of,
And wrungen out her tings and thot to dy.

'Nay, nay,' 'ol drageroony hym did say,
'Me eaten noten yooer, not no way,
Mayhap sum udder day, me ryght off colore.'
'Thank Goden all for that!' this lang-synce mayde
Replayed, 'here taken of this Renee
For your indigestyion.'

Drageroony quaffen on the cure at her suggestyion
An began to feel his betterun,
When all at once uppen rode
Geraint the Knight of the green crass code
An loppen off his headen.
Alas, alack, unwelladay!
(D'yer think he learnt his lessyion?)

Houndspeak Forever

Pheasants are truculent in thin birch
because it is the season of the shoot
and they are soon to be shot. Cartridges everywhere
like sawn-off crayons that always draw red.
We cared for birds once and loathed the spouting rifle.
Remember an albino broke cover
crossed our hearts
his colourless life had to continue
it was a matter of soul.

Birds are small-spirited and so were you eventually.
I like birds better for surviving
in prescribed ways or dying without recourse.
It ends in the sea, Houndspeak
a cauldron of dogs boiling alive
lifting the lead sky
slavering rain on our heads.
Holding in the rain was so good
to find warm flesh in wilderness.

Branches breaking from the starting up place
as if birds could be hard and trees hurt.
We walked to Houndspeak, boots thundering, words stripped
to nothing when nothing was a pleasure,
you made your blood move twice, an invincible aliveness
that cracked and kindled
brought lovers out of the air.
The difference is appalling.

Contrasts put a drool on the appetite.
We picked sticks and threw them for each other,
caught icicles. Early frost
had got in the living limbs
to still the sap, snap it off.
It shouldn't have been that cold.
You should have told me about death.
Your silence a pack of lies.
We heartily enjoyed the fire we made.

Bones are invested with the same importance.
I have found quite a few where pheasants fell unnoticed.
Nourishing blood found a way home,
feathers malingered awhile, almost indestructible
then turned to bracken
indistinguishable from other growths.
Not so bones,
bones are albino
the peg on which we hang our singularity.

Everything in nature prepared me for this
but not so the shotgun I took to your image.
Simple to take life
but a matter of speculation
how life allows itself to be taken.
I wish you had seen Houndspeak as I saw it this evening
the pink sun given and swallowed
and a moment's repletion.
The difference is appalling.

Dark

Call me a dealer in cold fish and flat bread
passing on what He gave in abundance

castigating myself to eat,
beat this Christ mass brittleness out.

Rejoice a Virgin is born of a Virgin.

Bad white snow stains the glass window,
lithely slips into Sligo's soil
where things get bred without me.

Wine cracks the chalice,
my raiments stand
stiff with cold
on their own.

Sweat of ages
fire to ice.

Candles sting in the hooding
and unhooding,
I burn the altar

shoddy as a moth

buttoned to the mouth.

Stuff it spills, vile believings,
ears I've filled with woodshavings.

My footprints sizzle, I go from church to bed and back
compelled to the confessional.

She comes three times this week
so steeped in sin
I smell the musk and tremble.

We dig dirt in the mole atmosphere,
share the same black velvet air.

My stopped eyes see
my fingers itch
for the contours of her, armfuls of cream

envious blood in motion

red sea rioting.

Priests were boys an age ago.

Fishes came to my hands
fresh from the lough
hot from the water.

With wrath I draw hot tears from her
and dry her up for Heaven.

When she is gone
I fear the dark.

Galway Bay

She ate the weeds off the shore,
filling her kids' bellies with a boiling potful.
Mick hadn't been seen for weeks,
it was rumoured he'd gone north after the beating
her father gave him.

She clung by the sea like a hunted animal
and the sea day by day tanned her skin more.
She was thirty and looked sixty,
her choice to drown or to drown.

And when her kids sent up one cry
of pain and of hunger
she turned them all in to be taken away,
her eyes so black by then they'd not heal,
her bones curling.

When the last of them,
the smallest baby with smudged and neutral cheeks,
had been removed from her arms,
she let out a curse that broke the sky
over Galway Bay.

Her life came home to her then,
and the lives other people were living
as she sat and sat and looked over to America.
And she couldn't for the life of her
choose heaven.

A travelling woman, she had her boots,
the proudest thing on her person,
but with the last of her strength she pulled
and gave them to the sea.

And she would not turn again to the land of her birth
and she would not walk on the water.

Ballygrand Widow

So, you have gone my erstwhile glad boy,
whose body, I remember, stained my big cream bed,
and didn't we mix the day and the night in our play,
we never got up for a week.

If I must set my alarm again,
and feed the hungry hens in the yard,
and draw the milk from my cow on time,
and skulk my shame down Ballygrand Street
to get a drink,
it'll not be for you I think,
but my next husband,
a fine cock he shall be.

So, you are no more in this town
my lovely schoolboy, and how the floss
of your chin tickled me.
And you swam your hands all over,
you shouted for joy, the first time.
Ah, my darling!

I wear your mother's spit on my shoes,
the black crow priest has been to beat me.
But you gave me a belly full, the best,
and they shan't take it.
The days are unkind after you, they are empty.
I lie in the sheets, the very same sheets;
you smelled sweeter than meadow hay.
My beautiful boy you have killed me.

Corrofin's Lament

Perdue.
You, my last hope, had my heart in ambush,
chose your twentieth year to spring this hare,
discontent.
But listen to your father
who swings a pitchfork and asks nothing
except the sun comes up, the hours of darkness sleep.

Perdition.
On your head disown the son, only one I had,
look on this patch of land, dear Clare, everything I have.
I believe in keeping close to the earth
and you a glutton want jazz-rhythms, ask for colour,
to go for a soldier or a sailor,
see the world,
I want you old before your time,
I want to leave myself behind.

Perfect.
These things are ordained by God,
the greatest patriarch of them all,
who wears a beard like a goat and deals severity
on his transgressing sons.
Once I'd have mashed you into the ground
with my fists that are clods.
Reason deserts me, my head also became a clod
from digging and scraping,
the gospel according to my father on earth
who lives in the earth, and approved nothing.

Plain.
A plain land and you see I am a plain person,
that is if you'd ever took the trouble to look at me
hard, you were always looking past to horizons
more imagined than real.
We lived without a woman, I never touched you again
except to knock you over.
It was my way with love.

Perhaps
you detected some solitude about my heart
as I kept it from you, a rotten potato,
that would, if not withdrawn, destroy the crop.
I believed in the plaster virgin, she seemed enough
to mother you, and the countrywoman who came
to dole your fare and scour our floor,
and replenish the saucer of holy water
you refused to wear, when entering and leaving
our home. She kept a straight face the while.

Progress
is what sticks in my mind from what you said
before you left, nothing moves in this place,
the few cows are statues, the stones don't walk,
the roads are bloodless veins, and twenty years ago
my appearance was unchanged.
I grew older sooner, under my father's strap,
used it in time to keep my trousers up
and tone your buttocks up.

Perish.
Can an old man ask for love?
I was like the stud bull, that's all,
my pride was in my balls, the globe of the world
to me, you left me to die as I lived
with my sleeves rolled to the elbows and boots
too tough to take off. I work to death in my sleep,
I die at the door, the threshold you passed over.
For the life of me I couldn't find a tear.
You did right for yourself son.

Mick Donahoe

Lovely Mick Donahoe was me daddy, a flower of a man,
sweet with his fists, they were the big knuckles
you see on trees that grow wrong,
that stand against the wind and grow wrong.

The biggest hands in Dublin belonged to me daddy
and the baddest reputation.
It hung around like animal stink
after he was gone, and he was always going,
north, south or over to England.

The faces he left mashed.
The world had got up against him before he was born,
box this, box that, he was always boxing
second only to boozing.

Look out.
We spent our little lives dodging him.
He came back but to kill or make another of us
or rearrange our mammy.
We had ideas about him, we were glad he died slow

and dumb,
there'd never been a word to get in over his roaring,
but at the end he was begging,
for an ear to come nearer
so he could say the thing about love
stricken from his tongue.

Finney's Bar

Ah, you rare old devil, you fine fellow Finney,
ravishing your fiddle so the tendons won't sing
of virginity's meaning, Finney, you dog
with your dead-born tunes,
elbows to the big bugger moon, in Dublin,
your backside afire as you saw at the throat,
and Irishman's Fancy is spilled.

Finney, you swore on your fathers, you'd kissed
the hem of her sky-blue dress,
emulsion-skinned holy mother whose waters
are breaking with sin and piss; and she unbandaged
her bleeding heart, she reeled
as you cut your fiddle,
and the boys in the backroom reeled with her.

Finney, I'll never forget you, a bless and a curse
on your head and the murder you did,
to music, the black and amber we passed together,
your white confessional walls,
they fell like snow on my head, Finney, you rogue,
I've looked up your trouser leg.
I'd die to drink with you again.

Gael Marian

You should see my life Holy Mother,
step down out of that candle cupboard.
I can just imagine you picking through
the cow dung in our yard. I needed
a drink or two to get through my life.
To be an Irishwoman is a raw deal,
did no Irishwoman tell you?
I can see you're not a drinking woman
in your complexion, which is so pure, so how
did you dirty yourself enough to have him?
Without spot or sin, now there's a neat trick.
I used to think your father in heaven
had raped you, same as my father on earth,
but you looked too happy. My baby also
was a boy who slipped out of me
in the fields one day, a bloody fledgling
with an old stunned face, and he's still there
in snow and sun, no trouble to anyone.

If I lay on my back in bed I can see
the blue mountains. Since the old one went
I'm all that's left and the sheets clot
with all the time I spend in bed, they smell
like rotten egg with unwashing.
I can't be bothered, I think of the beach,
wide and handsome, and powder under my toes
where I ran as a child knickerless into the sea.
There'll never be that time again, it hurts me maybe.
Yesterday I was a girl, hairless, blank,
where the wind blew my brains out.
I wish thinking had come to me, and anger,
sooner, but I ate flat bread, bad-mouthed none
and kept on the run, my best freedom
to race the wind off the sea.
I wish I was a sailor, to be a sailor
is ideal, not to belong is ideal.
Sailors own the world, the sailors
I've kissed who don't care for anyone.

Down to one cow hollering to have the milk
taken off, I pity her. The priests make more mess,
they hatch and hatch in this country,
they drop their messes on the head
of a poor woman, the priests I've kissed
who don't care for anyone.
I make my own music when I've had a few,
I make a party. They must hear me roaring
in heaven but I can't be bothered to gag.
The thing about you Holy Mother
is your silence, you don't have a tongue
or a temper, by the look of you
like the top of a sea I can't get into.
It doesn't worry me, most things are over,
most of my life has run in wax
through my fingers, those idle candles
we burnt between us.

Deborah Randall was born in 1957 in Gosport, Hampshire, and now lives in Kirkwall in the Orkneys. She worked in hotels, a plastics factory and a children's home before going to Sheffield University to study English, and only started writing three years ago.

In 1987 she won the Bloodaxe poetry competition and the £1000 Bridport poetry competition, and saw her poems published in Penguin's *Gregory Poems* anthology. Her prize in the Bloodaxe competition was £1000 plus the publication of her first book of poems. *The Sin Eater* is a Poetry Book Society Recommendation.